Spanish For Beginners

From Beginner To Expert

Marcus Rodriguez

2

professional before attempting any techniques outlined in this book.by reading this document, the reader agrees that under no circumstances is the author responsible for any losses, direct or indirect, which are incurred as a result of the use of information contained within this document, including, but not limited to, errors, omissions, or inaccuracies

TABLE OF CONTENTS

INTRODUCTION

Over the last several centuries, Spanish has been across multiple continents and forged connections between all of them. Spanish has persisted as a linguistic force since the Spanish empire began to cover the world over. The language spoken now isn't quite the same as the language spoken in the 15th century on the first voyage to the new world, but the similarities between that variety of Spanish and the modern-day variety of Spanish sets you up for libraries worth of literature from all over the world in the Spanish language.

What's more is the sheer beauty of the fact that Spanish, since it's covered the world over, has taken in a number of influences from other languages. Through its journey starting as a mere dialectical splinter of Vulgar Latin (the version of Latin spoken by the general populace of the Roman Republic and the Roman Empire), Spanish has picked up plenty of influences from all kinds of different languages and cultures, most notably from Arabic during the Arab occupation of Spain from the 700s to around the thirteenth century, but also from the Goths, the Basques, the Native Americans, and the Celts.

So, in other words, when you learn Spanish, you're setting yourself up to be involved in learning a whole wealth of cultural and historical information in what is a relatively passive manner. That sheer attachment to history is one of the most beautiful things about learning language in general.

However, there are a great number of reasons otherwise for which you might learn Spanish. The growth of the Latin American population and the dissemination of Latin American culture into the United States provide an excellent opportunity in two ways. Firstly, you will inevitably be a more attractive candidate for various careers from a perspective of qualifications. Your ability to speak Spanish will make you an asset in more ways than you can possibly fathom, and a huge number of companies will be lining up in order to get you to work with them, especially if you're specialized in another manner too.

Secondly, you'll have opened the door to talking to a whole new set of people. No longer will you be relegated to speaking simply to people who know and understand English; rather, you'll be able to speak to and with people from the culturally beautiful continents of South America and Central America and the wonderful Latin American people. It will also enable you to go to travel to Spain with ease and talk to numerous people who are native Spanish speakers and, more importantly, natives to the region, which will most certainly help you to understand the culture, customs, and realities of the place that you're in.

Due to many long stretches of communication with the British and as a result of normal antiquated progenitors, Spamish has offered English-speakers a genuinely simple way to bantering utilizing an alternate language. Spanish and English offer a few likenesses in sentence development. You may even understand that a great deal of Spanish and English words has comparable sounds. The restricted French sounds may in any case be natural to you in light of films and TV shows.

A portion of these one of a kind Spanish sounds incorporate the quiet "h" and the rough "r" sound; however, this doesn't totally imply that all that you watch and hear on TV is absolutely precise. In any case, having the option to receive the Spanish articulation you have procured from watching films can help you a great deal while learning the language.

Just like the English spoken in the United States, the English spoken in Australia, and the English spoken in England are vastly different, likewise is the Spanish of Spain, the Spanish of Mexico, and the Spanish of, say, Argentina. They're different in manner of accent and dialect and some basic things, such as the usage of "vosotros" in Castilian Spanish (Castellano), or the Spanish of mainland Spain, where instead "ustedes" is used in Latin American Spanish. There's also the fact that certain dialects use the pronoun vos, which is generally never used otherwise and sounds rather booky and antiquated in the same way that using the pronoun thou sound in English.

These dialects were made from the Latin language utilized by the Romans during their attacks in 1 B.C.; yet notwithstanding their normal root, the development of the Spanish language is not quite the same as the advancement of Italian and French (which despite everything share a great deal of similitudes even up to today).

This book contains demonstrated advances and methodologies on the best way to begin learning the Spanish language. I trust that through this book, you will pick up the certainty to begin learning another dialect, regardless of how old you are. Try not to stress on the off chance that you have not yet taken in any unknown dialect previously. In this book, you will locate the fundamental standards of the language which can make it simpler for you to assemble expressions and sentences in French. You will learn fundamental expressions, yet additionally French letters in order, sentence development, just as articulation. There are numerous explanations behind needing to become familiar with the Spanish language rapidly. You should locate the correct inspiration and wonder why you're keen on learning Spanish. Possibly you will travel soon, or you want to serve your locale better. It may be the case that you need to upgrade your resume or, just, to extend your points of view by getting a subsequent language. Whatever your reasons, learning Spanish can be a satisfying undertaking.

Interfacing with others and our condition is the way we took in our local dialects as infants. Likewise, tuning in and associating with people around us help structure our jargon and information. The explanation that connection works when learning another dialect is that it is basic, and it's common.

There is a hypothesis in language that when learning another dialect as an intuitive procedure between a student and a local speaker, correspondence and familiarity are handily accomplished. It is on the grounds that the local speaker adjusts the language and makes it simpler for you as an apprentice to become familiar with the language. The capable speaker will utilize known jargon, talking gradually and obviously. The local speaker will modify the point, stay away from sayings, and utilize less complex linguistic structures. Thusly, the information encourages you with a superior comprehension of the Spanish language.

With more than 400 million local Spanish speakers around the world, Spanish is the official language of 21 nations and is the second most-communicated in language on the planet! Remember that you should try sincerely and focus on concentrated investigation meetings to have the option to convey in Spanish rapidly. We start by setting a practical cutoff time and making a learning plan. When you have an arrangement set up, you should begin acquainting yourself with fundamental jargon words that you can later expand upon. Next, finding an online program, guide, class, or application that will give you access to both sound and visual learning. Having a decent blend of instructional materials will assist with keeping you responsible and on target. One of the most basic parts of rapidly learning another dialect is to inundate yourself in the language as much as possible. At long last, practice increasingly visit so you can speak in light of other Spanish speakers — keeping that the objective is to comprehend the Spanish language rather than simply deciphering it.

In this book, we will concentrate on furnishing you with words written in Spanish and English. These words will be utilized in a sentence in Spanish, which we will likewise convert into English with the goal that you can investigate the setting in the two dialects. Through this, you will have the option to look at the importance of every one of the words, concentrating on only each in turn.

For example:

Hola / Hello

Hola, ¿Cómo estas? / Hello, how are you?

Here, the main word is hola, which is the word initially mentioned, while the rest of the words are what we call context. Thanks to this method, you will learn to use the main word in context and also the meaning of the secondary words.

In the following lessons, you will find words from different topics, such as verbs, adjectives, adverbs, polysemous words, home, household chores, clothes, garments, accessories, nature, animals, professions, family, relationships, numbers, and many more. Learning these words and knowing how to use them will upgrade your Spanish language to the intermediate level.

Spanish has a very different system of pronunciation to English. It's far more regular but also a fair bit more nuanced in the specific sounds. With the espoused regularity of Spanish pronunciation comes a fair amount of adjustment from our English alphabet where a given letter can stand in for any number of different sounds.

We recommend reviewing the words provided here in the book at least once every two months so that you can remember them and put them into practice in your everyday life.

There are plenty of books on this subject on the market, so thank you again for choosing this one! Every effort was made to ensure it is full of as much useful information as possible. Please enjoy!

WORKING WITH A SPANISH GRAMMAR NARRATOR TO UNDERSTAND THE LANGUAGE

I am sure that you have at least gotten your feet wet regarding the Spanish language. Or you just need a few adjustments to get things in line, right?

To begin, you need to first understand what roles a narrator plays in your understanding and education of the Spanish language. To gain understanding, you may have to ask yourself who or what is a Spanish grammar narrator?

In brief, this is that person who talks or narrates to you about the specific grammar rules that must be observed when writing or speaking the language, and, in this context, they usually represent the grammar authors. Their role is assisting you in mastering the language. The method will enable you to grasp the proper Spanish language grammar to avoid immediate and future grammar errors.

On the other hand, a Spanish grammar narrator is an application that can be installed on your personal computer or phone. It has a pre-recorded voice that explains the different grammar rules. These apps also represent the views of the grammar authors and, in most cases, are reliable.

How a Spanish Grammar Narrator Helps You to Understand Spanish To enable you to understand Spanish better, a capable narrator helps you in the following ways:

A narrator makes the memorization of the grammar easy. Under normal circumstances, being talked to about something can stick longer in your memory than when reading it on paper. A narrator will help you to visualize the rules. For instance, it would be easier for you to remember the rules if you rewind a visual explaining the rules in your mind.

On the other hand, the application narrator also makes the memorization of the grammar easy for you. For example, you can rewind what you have forgotten over and over again. The visual part of the application is also helpful as it displays to you how and where to apply the rules, which makes it hard for you to forget.

A narrator makes the whole lesson easy to understand. A narrator will explain to you how to apply those grammar rules on your sentences and phrases. More often, they draw diagrams to explain when and how to use the different types of clauses. For instance, they would teach you in an illustrative manner where to position verbs, nouns, and quotations, among other things. The exciting thing about them is that they are real, so you can see them with your eyes and feel their emotions. You can also ask them a question if you want. Unlike other sources, such as a textbook, you do not work on your own even if you do not understand anything.

They teach you the grammar rules that you need to learn. For you to effectively speak, listen, and read in Spanish, you have to be good in the grammar part. A narrator goes into detail to explain all the concepts concerning grammar that needs to be in place. They teach you step-by-step, explaining to you the various relations between the different parts of speech, which you could have ignored if you were left to your own devices. This makes the learning process easy, and it also reduces the time you would need to perfect your skills since you start developing them from the start.

They inspire you to perfect your skills. Use the services of a narrator to train you to improve your work. They go into detail when explaining to you the grammar rules. That is from the simple ones to the complex ones. This kind of training makes you a better learner since you are supervised. This makes you a better learner since most new languages require such an approach to crack them. As such, they can be good aspirators and source of motivation.

Qualities of an Efficient Spanish Grammar Narrator

They are lively. A compelling narrator needs to have a warm attitude. This will enable them to present the content effectively. Also, an energetic performer inspires their audience and makes it easy for them to ask questions in case of any need. Furthermore, they facilitate learning since the same effect passes on to the audience who appreciate having the lesson in grammar.

On the other hand, a grammar narrator application that is interactive allows more students to gain insight into the grammar rules. For it to be effective, it needs to incorporate the visual component, as well as the audio element that goes hand in hand. For instance, when a noun or verb is spelled in audio, its visual parts need to appear so that the learner can connect the two. Anything presented in audio needs to be accompanied by the corresponding visual component.

A narrator uses body gestures and expressions to a point. An efficient narrator uses any available tool or creativity to drive their point home. Therefore, they should not shy away from expressing what they are talking about using their body language or expressions. For example, the learner can construct phrases concerning bodily actions such as hugging if the narrator uses the right gesture. They need to show the action in order to cement the idea on the learner's mind. In doing so, the learner would vividly remember their actions when they encounter structures requiring the use of the grammar rules for such actions.

The tutor needs to have all the teaching or guiding aids. Things such as exercises, illustrations, and whiteboards, among other accessories, are a necessity for an effective grammar narrator. These enable them to offer quality explanations that can be easily remembered by the learners. For instance, they need the whiteboard to illustrate the various rules and syntaxes to follow and how they relate to each other. They would also use the pen to draw images to explain the various types of interrelations between the variables. With that said, it's vital for the tutor to have various teaching aids that will support students in their quest to learn how to speak Spanish.

How to Find a Spanish Grammar Narrator

Human Grammar Narrator

To find a human grammar narrator for your leaning needs, you can utilize two methods: Search for them manually. Spanish grammar narrators, in most cases, can be found in most countries across the globe. Ask around where you can find them. If there is no one who can offer such services, you may require referrals. Alternatively, you can visit different bureaus and consultants. If you do not find anyone around your area, you can either migrate to another location, in places where they can be found. Or migrate to any Spanish-speaking country where the probabilities of finding one are high.

Search for them through the internet. With the availability of the World Wide Web, you can quickly get in touch with an online narrator within seconds. What you need is a high-speed internet connection, apart from a personal computer.

Google the term "online grammar narrator." You will get a lot of choices to choose from. Take a look at the interesting ones then decide. Alternatively, you can ask for referrals from your current tutor or fellow learners and then enroll with them. Some of them might require paid subscriptions, while others are for free. Choose what suits you best.

Application Grammar Narrator

To find a suitable one, you can do the following:

Ask for referrals for a better option. You can ask your friends which applications they are using if any. If not, ask your coach or tutor the same question, and they would provide you with the appropriate answer.

Check reviews. To get a suitable application for your narration, you can go online and check the available narrators. After noting a few that interests you, go ahead and search for a review about them. To perform this, just type the name of the application and the word "review" on a browser. Several results would appear. Go over them and see what other people talk about some of the apps that you want to install as your narrator. Go for the one that has top reviews. Remember also to check if they require some subscription fee or not. Take it from a friend. Alternatively, you can share one from your friend's device. Modern electronics such as smartphones, tablets, and personal computers have applications that can enable the sharing of software. Therefore, if your friend, tutor, or colleague has an app that meets your learning needs, ask them to share it with you.

Working with a Grammar Narrator to Understand Spanish

After getting your ideal grammar narrator, it's time to start working with them. Here are the different ways you can work with them.

Face-to-face narrator

For this kind of narrator, you need to be in the same physical environment. These could be in a hall, class, or office. Therefore, make sure that you proceed to the agreed venue equipped with the necessary learning materials. This includes things such as pens, papers, and books, among other accessories required for such type of engagements.

Listen to them keenly as they explain the various aspects of grammar. If you have any burning question within the learning session, ask them immediately to avoid any confusion since the instructions will continue to progress, which can disadvantage you. After understanding the provided explanation to your question, you can tell them to proceed with the narration. Keep repeating the same process for every presentation.

Online narrator

For this kind of narrator, you need to login into your device then open the internet. Such presentations could either be live or recorded sessions. For a live performance, tune in at the required time and watch as the narrator presents his or her instructions concerning grammar. Take notes concerning the essential details that you need to understand. In case it is an offline presentation, log in it to your machine at your convenient time, and start watching the performance. Do the same things as the online presentation.

Application grammar narrator

With this type, open the necessary application and start gaining insights concerning the grammar rules. Most of these applications allow you to navigate through them. Therefore, if you have forgotten any important lesson, you can rewind and replay the app once again.

Find Your Voice

"Learning another language is not only learning different words for the same things, but learning another way to think about things." - Flora Lewis

"I enjoy translating; it's like opening your mouth and hearing someone else's voice emerge." - Iris Murdoch

One of my earliest memories happened at a park when I was about five years old. Two women on a bench were speaking with each other in a foreign language. I was amazed: They seemed to be communicating, and yet to my young English-speaking ears, it sounded like complete gibberish.

In the car on the way home, I proposed a theory to my parents. Perhaps to those foreign women, English also sounds like complete gibberish, with the exact same sonic effect on their ears. If this were true, languages would be like radio stations, each one sounding like indefinite, neutral static to someone who is not tuned in.

But this isn't quite true. To Spanish speakers, English doesn't sound like Portuguese or German. It sounds like English. Rather than sounding like random nonsense, it actually has a voice of its own, even to people who don't understand it.

In fact, every language has its own distinct sound. For example, even if you don't know a word of Mandarin or Arabic, you can easily learn to tell the two apart just by the way they sound.

This Spanish "sound" is part of the foundation we'll be laying here at the beginning of Lesson 1.

But we won't be able to talk about the sound of the language without also covering the personality of the language.I moved to Argentina a year after I started learning Spanish. While there, I made many new friends with whom I only spoke in Spanish. But during the first three months, I didn't feel like myself.

The version of me that my Argentinian friends knew was a brand-new creation. They saw a different side of me, a different voice and personality, that none of my friends at home had ever known. This was the Spanish-language version of me. It forced me to express myself very differently than I was used to doing.

When I speak Spanish, many of the quirky idiosyncrasies of my own personality are lost. Since I was raised speaking English, my personality is intertwined with the English language. But the Spanish rendition of myself is not a lot like my English-speaking personality. At first, it was like bad movie subtitles that don't really express the original meaning.

But at the same time, the Spanish language has its own idiosyncrasies. During my time in Argentina, I began to develop new stories, jokes, and personality traits in this language, all of which were all entirely separate from my English-speaking personality. I had opened up a new side of my mind that I never knew existed. By learning Spanish, I discovered a whole new amazing world that I could live in, entirely hidden from my native tongue.It's time for you to start building that world. And speaking of your native tongue, the "tongue" is a good place to start.

The Spanish Voice

It's tempting to think that Spanish speakers were born with a different variety of tongue or voice box. They make certain sounds that we never produce in English.

But it's simply not true. Spanish speakers' vocal and oral apparatuses are physically identical to those of English speakers.

The difference is in the language itself.

Let's do a quick exercise to demonstrate. Here I've listed a few names that are quite common in Spanish-speaking countries and are also well-known to English speakers.

If you were to read these names off in an English voice, they would sound extremely different from the Spanish way of saying them.

But on the other hand, if you go to the effort to pronounce a Spanish speaker's name the correct way, the way he or she has said it and heard it his/her whole life, it's a big compliment to them. They'll be honored and will feel a much closer connection to you.

Bottom line: If you truly want to communicate on a personal level, it's much more than just saying the right words. How you say those words makes an enormous difference.

We'll work on that Spanish voice soon, but we have to go a little deeper. Before we can produce accurate Spanish sounds, we need to think about Spanish more deeply than that.

A new language doesn't just sound different. It thinks differently.

"Named Must Your Voice Be Before Brandish It You Can."

Look again at the names listed above. If you were to hear a bilingual person reading them over and over, first in a Spanish voice and then in an English voice, it would sound as if she were two different actors reading the same script.

In fact, the term "actor" is a good analogy for language learning. When you switch into a different language, it's not just your voice that should change. There are other aspects of communication that require a different mindset.

If you've worked on learning a language before, you may be used to studying grammar, vocabulary, and idioms separately. But what you're about to learn will turn them all into one entity.

Let's imagine for a second that you decide to talk like Yoda from Star Wars. Instead of saying "Your fear must be named before you can banish it," Yoda says, "Named must your fear be before banishing it you can."

He mixes up the word order in a strange way. But hey, it's Yoda. It's part of his personality.

If you start imitating Yoda on purpose, you might find that you start to think differently as well. Your personality will change slightly based on what you're saying.

But for efficiency, we're going to go the opposite direction: We're going to change our personality first.

For the Star Wars fans, I'm afraid Yoda isn't quite going to do the job. We need to create a very unique personality, something that really encompasses everything about the Spanish language. It has to be a person separate from yourself, but you have to be able to switch back and forth between your own personality and that separate personality.

our Spanish personality is a bee named Joel.

Joel talks kind of like Yoda, but he follows his own strange rules about it.

Let's take an example from the Spanish verb for "liking" something. In these situations, the grammar is completely reverse that of English. The subject and the object are switched. There's no literal way to say "I like tea" in Spanish; instead, Joel always says me gusta el té, which literally means "to me is pleasing the tea".

This confuses a lot of English speakers. Even after they've learned the grammar and memorized loads of phrases, it can be all too easy to make a silly mistake with this verb.

But I make it simple. When I'm Timothy, my English self, I "like" things. It's something I do: It's my opinion of the tea, my own action.

However, when I'm Joel, my Spanish self, I don't "like" things. In my Joel personality, I'm too lazy to "like" things.

Joel doesn't want to be the one doing the action; instead, he wants the thing itself to do the action. He wants the tea to do the work for him.

So instead of saying "I like tea", Joel says "The tea is pleasing to me." Notice how Joel makes it sound like the tea is the one that's doing the action.

This is automatic for me when I switch into my Spanish personality. I don't have to think about it. It's a part of who I am, as Joel.

Now you have to become the bee.

You need to associate everything you learn about Spanish with Joel. Each time you come across a new Spanish word, idiom, or grammar rule, you can associate it with Joel, and it will become a part of your developing Spanish personality.

Let's begin by learning some more things about Joel.

Putting on Your Wings

When you get your Joel character on, you'll want to understand everything about Joel, including the world that he lives in. So, before we can become the bee, we have to stop and get to know him really well. Pay close attention and try to remember every detail of his personality.

First of all, Joel is no mere human bee. He's not even from Earth.

He lives on a planet called "Yol". If you think about it, "Yol" sounds kind of like "Joel", and in fact Joel sometimes gets his own name confused with the name of the planet he lives on because they sound kind of similar.

Joel is a mischievous bee. While he tries to appear attractive and charming, he really just uses his wealth for his own selfish purposes, and he tries to get everyone else to do work for him because he's extremely lazy.It's important to note that Joel's tastes are pretty strange: He loves drinking tea, and he'll do almost anything to get a nice hot cup. But he has a strong distaste for all mammals (that is, animals with fur such as dogs, horses, bears, and giraffes); in fact, he's generally frightened of all such animals.

However, his best friend is a lizard. He has no problem with him, because he's a reptile, not a mammal. As you'll see in future stories, this lizard has no name, can't talk, and likes to spend time in dark caves.

Joel also hangs out with a group of stuffed pandas. They're OK because they aren't real pandas; they're living stuffed animals, which is not a problem by Joel's strange standards.

Since the pandas are clumsy and simple-minded, Joel loves causing mischief to these stuffed pandas. He thinks it's funny when they get dizzy or blown around by wind, which happens pretty often.

Also be aware that Joel has a tendency to get into a strange sort of mood and to talk with an old-fashioned, almost formal British mode of speech. This especially happens when he's about to do something mischievous, so be on the lookout for that. If he starts speaking in a pompous voice, it usually means that he's up to no good.

Another funny thing about the way that Joel talks is that he can be extremely redundant. He'll say the same thing more than once in a sentence, sometimes even to the point of bad logic, such as double negatives, like "I didn't see nothing".

We absolutely must imitate this kind of thing if we want to speak like Joel authentically. It may be uncomfortable or feel wrong, but just remember that you aren't the one saying "I didn't see nothing"; it's just Joel, and it makes perfect sense for him.

VOCABULARY

When you think about vocabulary, is the first impression that comes to mind those vocabulary tests you had at school, where all you did was memorize a certain list of words for each test and forget everything as soon as you were done?

What a stressful, ineffective way of learning vocabulary! This was one of the key reasons I wanted to avoid learning a new language, and I'm sure you can relate to that. So how can we learn vocabulary differently?

The first visual that comes to mind is a dictionary. We live in an era where free dictionaries can be found online. What's more, it's easier than ever to search for a word and its definition, or how it's used in your target language; plus, we can find examples of this word in context. That's so convenient, isn't it?

But what if you're not into dictionaries? Are you shaking your head in disapproval as you read these lines? Fortunately, a dictionary isn't the only way to improve your vocabulary. It's a tool to turn to when in we're in need, not something we should open up and study, like a textbook.

If we all know someone who speaks our target language—be it a friend or a family member—then we have access to new vocabulary more frequently. If we live in a country where people speak our target language, then new vocabulary is everywhere. We often don't even have to look for it.

But how is it possible to find new vocabulary to learn online for free? And how do you make all that new vocabulary stick?

Let's dive right in now.

REPETITION, REPETITION, REPETITION

"Review your vocabulary," your language teacher used to say. "There's a test coming up."

"Time to go over the formulas again," advised the science teacher before handing you a new set of exercises to do. Teachers generally insist on reviewing what you've learned. And they're absolutely right!

Our brains love repetition because it helps new concepts stick and solidifies new memories. That's why professional basketball players make hundreds or thousands of shots per day to improve their shooting percentage. It's why musicians practice scales over and over again. To make sure the new information stays fresh in your mind, you need to review it from time to time; otherwise, it'll l most likely vanish.

This is where the Spaced Repetition System (SRS) comes in. It's a method that gives you the new information before you can forget it so that it's always there when you need it. That way you can memorize new words and phrases and never forget them! How does that work?

When you find the right time interval between each recall, you can remember more by spending less time studying. Rather than cramming it all once and repeating it as often as possible, you distribute your efforts over time in a way that the information always stays active in your head. You can either find the right intervals yourself through practice, or you can have SRS software calculate them for you.Let's see how we can use SRS to learn vocabulary for free.

FLASHCARDS

Flashcards are pieces of paper with a word or a phrase in your target language written on one side and its translation in your native language on the other. To study them, you review both sides. Let's look at one example of how you can use flashcards to learn vocabulary.

First, create flashcards with the new words you want to learn. Use small pieces of paper so that you can easily flip them. Write each word or phrase in your target language on one side and the translation in your native language on the other.

Use separate boxes or designated spaces so that you can put the flash cards there before and after you review them. Each box represents a different time interval. For example, in one box you'll put the flash cards you want to review every day, another box for every other day, one for every week, and so on. The more easily you can remember a flashcard, the less often you'll have to review it.

Start by putting all the flashcards in a one box. This will be the box where you'll store all the new flash cards you haven't reviewed yet.

Take the first flashcard, look at the side of your native language, and try to think of its translation in your target language. It's more effective to test yourself on your target language rather than your own, especially if you want to learn how to speak or write in your target language. If you just want to understand a language, then do it the other way around.If you successfully remember the translation, move it to the next box (the one with the shortest time interval); if you don't remember it, the card remains in the first box. Then review the box with the shortest time interval, and if you get a card right, move it to the next box. If you fail to recall it, send it back to the first box, no matter which box it was in before.

Repeat the process until all the flashcards end up in the same box, the one containing everything you can successfully remember.

You can use flashcards not only for vocabulary, but also for anything else you wish to memorize, like grammar rules if you like learning about them.

Flashcards are easy to create and you can take them everywhere. Just organize them into decks and take some with you while you're waiting somewhere or when you're on the bus, etc.

Fortunately, that's just the analog way of going about SRS. If you choose to go the digital way, there's a lot of software out there to help you. Most apps and sites for vocabulary are based on SRS, and they calculate your spacing schedule for you so that you don't spend too much time figuring out how often you should review the new vocabulary. Let's look at some examples of SRS-based software.

ANKI

Anki is one of the most popular SRS software out there, including among language learners. With Anki, you import ready-made decks of cards with new words to learn or create your own, and the system quizzes you on them. If you remember a card well, you can ask Anki to test you much later on it. If you got it right but it wasn't so easy, you can ask to review it a bit more often. The harder it is for you to remember a card, the more often Anki will show it to you. If you get a card right over and over again, the time interval will increase and you won't see it again any time soon. If you can't remember a card well, Anki may ask you again, even during the same study session. Anki is free everywhere, except on the iPhone, but there are other free alternatives if you have an iPhone (check out Brainscape or Tinycards, which have similar features to Anki).

MEMRISE

Memrise is a platform (and an app) that has language learning courses designed to help you learn vocabulary. There are courses in many languages, and you can choose what appeals to you the most. For each new word or phrase, you can create your own memes so that you can remember them easier, and you can also create your own courses where you can import any words and phrases you want to learn. Memrise uses SRS to determine how often you should review the new pieces of vocabulary. There's a free and a paid version, but the free version is more than enough to get you going. The downside is that you don't have full control over what words you learn, but you can solve this by creating your own course in the platform.

DUOLINGO

Duolingo is a site that teaches languages for free and gamifies the whole process. All you have to do is choose the language you want to learn and start translating words and phrases the course gives you to improve your use of the language. The more you advance, the harder the sentences get. You continue until you finish the whole course and get a grasp on the language you want to learn. Duolingo can help you learn new vocabulary in a fun way. It can also teach you to study every day by awarding you points, and by letting you know if you're on a streak and how many days you've been learning.

I tried this platform for Spanish for a few months after it came out, and it taught me to learn something new in my target language every day and to have fun, but it wasn't enough for me. Because of that I looked for other methods to use at the same time. Just like on Memrise, the downside is that you don't have full control of what you learn, and Duolingo gives you phrases that you may find useless and uninteresting; however, if you don't learn them, you can't advance in the course.

CLOZEMASTER

Clozemaster is an online resource that helps you build your vocabulary and learn new words and sentences in context. It's designed like a video game, and has exercises where you have to choose or fill in the missing word. It's available as an app for smartphones and tablets, and as an online website. While this resource is suitable only for upper beginner or intermediate level learners, it's quite addictive and fun to use. You can easily learn lots of new words in context and even collect useful phrases, but, as with Memrise and Duolingo, you don't have full control here either. There's a free version you can use indefinitely, and it's available in a wide range of languages – even Guarani or Latin.So now that you have a few examples to consider, how do you make the most out of SRS software and gain full control of what you learn?

BECOMING THE MASTER OF YOUR SRS

As we saw, Anki and Memrise let you create your own flashcards and courses. Since this takes more time, you might be tempted to use the tons of ready-made flash cards and courses you can find on these platforms. The problem is that a lot of them come without context; they're just isolated words and phrases. Although you'll be able to remember them successfully, it's highly unlikely you'll use them while speaking the language.

To get the most out of SRS programs, you have to think of them as a place where you can insert your own words and phrases to learn—a white wall waiting for you to paint it the way you want so that you can use it.

By doing it this way, you can choose phrases that you know you'll eventually use when speaking, or new words in context. You can find that material by using the methods we earlier talked about collecting language material.

Do you want to speak about your favorite hobby? Create a deck of flashcards or a course with all the possible phrases you could use to talk about it, and let the software help you remember everything. Want to learn new words from an interesting article you read and put them to use? Copy the sentences where you found the words and put them in a new course with the article's title as a name.

Conversation - Dialogues

¡Subjuntivo, Loli, Subjuntivo!

De niña, eso es lo que a Loli le daba más vergüenza. Sus padres eran de España, pero ella era la peor de la clase de español: la que nunca recordaba los verbos irregulares, la que siempre confundía ser y estar, la que no entendía la diferencia entre por y para, la que nunca usaba el subjuntivo.

-¡A ver, Loli, ahora te toca a ti! —le decía la maestra, la Señorita Martina, que acababa de escribir en la pizarra una frase en español:

Espero que...

A la Señorita Martina le gustaba escribir frases inacabadas en la pizarra y luego pedir a los estudiantes que las completasen. Decía que era un método muy bueno para aprender gramática.

El problema era que Loli no tenía mucha imaginación y nunca se le ocurría nada interesante que decir.

Como ella no decía nada, poco a poco se fueron alzando las manos de los otros chicos de la clase:

-Espero que este año haga buen tiempo. —dijo Pete.

-Espero que mi madre venga. —dijo otro niño.

-Espero que vayamos a la playa en verano. —dijo Rose.

-Espero que tengas suerte. —dijo alguien más.

Como de costumbre, todos en la clase de español sabían qué decir. Todos excepto ella. Loli se estaba poniendo cada vez más nerviosa. Tenía que decir algo, pero no se le ocurría nada interesante. Finalmente, cerró los ojos, abrió la boca y dijo, en voz muy baja:

-¡Espero que él vuelve!

Todos los chicos de la clase se echaron a reír.

La Señorita Martina pensó "es un caso perdido. No hay nada que hacer. Esta niña es tonta", pero no dijo nada; simplemente se dio media vuelta, fue hacia la pizarra y escribió en letras muy grandes:

Vuelva

Luego, mirando hacia Loli, añadió en voz baja:

- Subjuntivo, Loli, subjuntivo...

La profe se había puesto triste. Parecía resignada. No dijo nada, pero todos en la clase se habían dado cuenta de lo que la Señorita Martina estaba pensando en aquel momento: que Loli era la niña más tímida de la clase, probablemente la niña más tímida que jamás hubiera existido.

Vocabulary:

Eso es lo que a Loli le daba más vergüenza: that´s what Loli was most embarrassed about

La que nunca recordaba los verbos irregulares: the one who never remembered the irregular verbs

Ahora te toca a ti: now it´s your turn

Nunca se le ocurría nada interesante que decir: it never occurred to her anything interesting to say

Poco a poco se fueron alzando las manos: little by little hands were being raised (put up)

Loli se estaba poniendo cada vez más nerviosa: Loli was getting more and more nervous

En voz muy baja: with a very low voice

Se echaron a reír: (they) burst out laughing

Es un caso perdido: (She) is a hopeless case

Se dio media vuelta: (She) turned

La pizarra: the whiteboard

Parecía resignada: (She) looked resigned

Se habían dado cuenta de: (They) had realized that

Un Pueblo Español

Loli no salía mucho.

Durante la semana ayudaba a su madre en las tareas de la casa. Planchaba la ropa de su padre y de su hermano, lavaba los platos después de comer, iba a hacer la compra todos los días, fregaba el suelo, limpiaba el polvo...

Como no tenía amigos, el fin de semana se quedaba en casa.

Y en casa Loli se aburría. No había mucho que hacer.

En su casa solo había tres libros. Tres libros que ya se conocía casi de memoria. Eran unos cuentos infantiles que su abuelo le había regalado cuando ella era todavía una niña. Estaban escritos en español y ella no entendía nada, pero le gustaba mirar las ilustraciones e imaginarse la historia mientras comía patatas fritas y bebía gazosa. Le encantaba comer patatas fritas de bolsa y beber gazosa mientras leía o mientras veía la televisión.

Cuando se aburría, veía la tele y comía patatas fritas; cuando se aburría de ver la tele, escuchaba música en la radio y comía patatas fritas; cuando se aburría de escuchar música se ponía a registrar los cajones de la casa, en busca de cualquier objeto para entretenerse un rato.

Fue así que un día descubrió el álbum de fotos viejas de su abuelo. Le gustaba mirarlas de vez en cuando y estudiar todos los detalles de cada escena: la gente que pasaba por la calle y que salía en la foto sin darse cuenta; la silla donde un viejo estaba sentado al sol; un perro que husmeaba la pared, las hojas de los árboles, la puerta de madera de una casa blanca con paredes de cal, unos niños sucios jugando despreocupados en la plaza...

Le gustaba observar los ojos de la gente, estudiar sus expresiones y preguntarse qué estarían pensando en aquel momento, qué les pasaba por la cabeza, cómo eran sus vidas. Le daba miedo pensar que muchos de ellos ya estarían muertos o serían muy viejos.

De entre todas aquellas fotos, la que más le llamaba la atención era una foto en blanco y negro de una vieja estación de tren.

Loli había visto esa foto muchas veces.

Parecía el andén de una de esas estaciones pequeñas de uno de esos pueblos olvidados de España donde nunca parecía pasar nada. Uno de esos pueblos de casas blancas, calles estrechas y empedradas, donde la gente era muy pobre y tenía que vivir de lo poco que cultivaban en el campo.

Loli acercó los ojos a la foto y se puso a estudiar a la gente que había en el andén. Había unos viejos con bastón sentados en un banco al sol. Probablemente iban allí todos los días a tomar el sol, ver pasar los trenes y observar con curiosidad a los viajeros que llegaban o partían.

Los niños a esa hora seguramente estaban en la escuela. Las mujeres en casa, preparando el almuerzo. Los hombres tal vez en el campo, trabajando, o quizás en el bar del pueblo, posiblemente el único bar del pueblo, haciendo lo que los hombres de antes solían hacer mejor: jugar a las cartas, fumar tabaco negro, beber vasos de vino peleón, hablar del tiempo y quejarse de la última cosecha de patatas, que fue terrible por culpa de la sequía.

Seguramente era un pueblo donde solo quedaban viejos y niños, pensaba Loli. La mayoría de los jóvenes se habrían ya marchado muy lejos en busca de una vida mejor. Quizás a la ciudad, o tal vez aún más lejos, al extranjero. Eran los años sesenta, los años duros de la emigración española.

Loli sabía que en esos años muchos españoles tuvieron que escapar de la miseria de España.

Vocabulary:

Planchaba: (she) used to iron

Fregaba el suelo, limpiaba el polvo: (she) used to mop the floor, wipe off dust

Se quedaba en casa: (she) stayed at home

Patatas fritas de bolsa: crisps

Cuando se aburría de ver la tele: when she got bored of watching telly

Se ponía a registrar los cajones de la casa: (she) started to rummage in the drawers of the house

En busca de cualquier objeto para entretenerse un rato: looking for any object to keep herself occupied for a while

El álbum de fotos viejas: the old-pictures album

Un perro que husmeaba la pared: a dog that was sniffing at the wall

Despreocupados: carefree

Le llamaba la atención: (it) used to draw her attention

El andén: the platform

Tenía que vivir de lo poco que cultivaban en el campo: (people) had to make a living out of what little produce they could grow in the field

Se puso a estudiar a la gente que había en el andén: (she) started to watch closely the people on the platform

Bastón: walking stick

Seguramente: probably, likely

Fumar tabaco negro: to smoke black tobacco

Vino peleón: cheap wine

Quejarse de la última cosecha de patatas: to complain about the last potato harvest

La sequía: the drought

Algo para adelgazar

La casa del mago estaba llena de gente.

-Do you have something to lose weight? Something good to lose weight fast? (¿Tiene algo para adelgazar? Algo que sirva para perder peso rápidamente). —dijo su madre en voz alta, nada más entrar.

Todos se giraron hacia ellas. Primero miraron a su madre, luego a ella.

Loli se puso roja. Sacó del abrigo una bolsa de patatas fritas con sabor a queso y se llevó una a la boca. Le daba vergüenza cuando la gente la miraba. Y cuando le daba vergüenza algo, se ponía a comer patatas fritas. No lo podía evitar.

El mago no dijo nada. Miraba a aquella mujer delgadísima, casi transparente, y parecía no comprender. Parecía que pensara "¿Esta mujer quiere adelgazar aún más?"

Era un tipo calvo, de unos 45 años, con gafas y bigote. Loli pensó que se parecía a Groucho Marx.

-It´s not for me, it´s for my daughter. (No es para mí, es para mi hija). –aclaró su madre, sonriendo coqueta, como si hubiera leído los pensamientos del mago. Estaba claro que a ella no le hacía falta adelgazar. Entonces el mago miró a Loli de arriba abajo, estudiándola en silencio.

Ella trató de esconder la bolsa de patatas fritas que llevaba en la mano, pero era demasiado tarde. El tipo que se parecía a Groucho Marx ya la había visto.

Tampoco ahora dijo nada, pero parecía estar de acuerdo con su madre. Loli pensó que la miraba como si pensase: "Sí, es verdad, esta chica necesita adelgazar urgentemente."

Loli se puso aún más roja.

-Sorry, but I was here before! (¡Perdone, pero yo estaba antes!) –dijo en voz alta una de las mujeres que había en la cola.

Su madre, que tenía la costumbre de saltarse la fila cuando iba de compras, fingió no haberla oído.

La señora de la fila insistió:

-You are the last one, madam! You have to queue like everybody else! (¡Usted ha llegado la última, señora! Tiene que hacer cola como todos).

Su madre, como quien oye llover, la ignoró y continuó hablando con el mago:

- A magic potion! (¡Una poción mágica!)

Loli se dio cuenta de que la mujer de la cola las miraba a su madre y a ella de reojo.

El resto de las personas que había en la casa posiblemente también las observaban, curiosas.

Loli se quería morir y no se atrevía a levantar la vista del suelo.

-Madam, we don´t make miracles here. What your daughter needs to do is to stop eating so much! (Señora, aquí no hacemos milagros. ¡Lo que su hija tiene que hacer es dejar de comer tanto!) –dijo finalmente el tipo que se parecía a Groucho Marx.

Las personas en la casa se echaron a reír.

Al final, el mago le vendió a su madre una infusión de hierbas que prometía quitar las ganas de comer. Eran un poco caras, pero valía la pena intentarlo.

Según su madre, si estuviera delgada podría echarse novio. Si se echase novio, sería feliz.

Vocabulary:

Llena de gente: full of people

Nada más entrar: as soon as (they) went in

Se giraron hacia ellas: (they) turned toward them

Loli se puso roja: loli went red

Con sabor a queso: cheese-flavoured (crisps)

Cuando le daba vergüenza algo, se ponía a comer patatas fritas: when she was embarrassed about something, she started to eat crisps.

Applying the Main Principles to Learning and Memorizing Spanish Vocabulary

First, I create a folder and then create multiple Excel files. Excel works the best because it eliminates the need to build a table. However, you can just as easily build a table using Microsoft Word, Pages or other word-processing software you happen to be using.

In this case, the files you need to create correspond to the letters of the Spanish alphabet. Below is an example of the alphabet with my locations:

A = Aberdeen Mall

B = Brandonhurst Elementary School

C = Carpet World

D = Maintstreet Downtown

E = Eric's House

F = Feurigstraße

G = Dad's Garage

H = Hospital

45

I = Ice Rink

J = Jasmine's House

K = Kirk's House

L = Lyle's House

M = Manny's House

N = Nolene's House

Ñ = Natalie's House

O = Olympic Stadium

P = Philipinnenstraße

Q = Quinn's House

R = Rick's House

S = Sahali Mall

T = Trevor's House

U = University Library

V = Varsity Movie Theatre

W = Wicklow Movie Theatre

X = Kane's House

Y = Yorkville Movie Theatre

Z = Zara's House

Name		Date Modified	Size	Kind
▶ 📁 A		Today 21:17	--	Folder
▶ 📁 B		Today 21:17	--	Folder
▶ 📁 C		Today 21:17	--	Folder
▶ 📁 D		Today 21:17	--	Folder
▶ 📁 E		Today 21:17	--	Folder
▶ 📁 F		Today 21:17	--	Folder
▶ 📁 G		Today 21:17	--	Folder
▶ 📁 H	Don't forget to make	Today 21:17	--	Folder
▶ 📁 I	a folder for ñ	Today 21:17	--	Folder
▶ 📁 J		Today 21:17	--	Folder
▶ 📁 K		Today 21:17	--	Folder
▶ 📁 L		Today 21:17	--	Folder
▶ 📁 M		Today 21:17	--	Folder
▶ 📁 N		Today 21:17	--	Folder
▶ 📁 ñ		**Today 21:19**	--	**Folder**
▶ 📁 O		Today 21:18	--	Folder
▶ 📁 P		Today 21:18	--	Folder
▶ 📁 Q		Today 21:18	--	Folder
▶ 📁 R		Today 21:18	--	Folder
▶ 📁 S		Today 21:18	--	Folder
▶ 📁 T		Today 21:18	--	Folder
▶ 📁 U		Today 21:18	--	Folder
▶ 📁 V		Today 21:18	--	Folder
▶ 📁 W		Today 21:18	--	Folder
▶ 📁 X		Today 21:18	--	Folder
▶ 📁 Y		Today 21:18	--	Folder
▶ 📁 Z		Today 21:18	--	Folder

It is very important that you have at least 10 stations assigned to each of the Memory Palaces you have selected based on locations with which you are very familiar. Remember, design your passage from station to station in such a way that you do not cross your own path and so that you do not trap yourself. You always want to leave yourself with the ability to add another 10 stations in each location.

Keep in mind that 10 stations are a number for right now. Later you can later expand to as many stations as you like per Memory Palace.

As you are trying to come up with each location to link with each letter, let yourself relax. Your mind has the perfect associations for you so long as you don't force it. If you can't think of something that is totally fitting, such as Wicklow for W, just let your mind do its work and go with whatever feels right.

You do not want odd or awkward associations that cause you to stumble in your thinking. You want the associations to be natural so that you can move fluidly through your mind when searching for the words you have remembered.

When it comes to speaking and understanding what you hear, you will sometimes need to do this in real time, so it is very important not to hinder yourself by using forced associations that you will forget and struggle to work back into your memory. That will take the fun out of everything.

Now, let me show you how I have used just two letters: A and E.

Aberdeen Mall

For A, which is Aberdeen Mall, my first ten stations are:

Entrance

Jewelry store

Bookstore

Escalator

Food court

Shoe store

Grocery store entrance

Movie theatre entrance

Mall Exit

Parking lot

Amar

The first "A" word I would like to learn is perhaps the most important: amar. Amar means to love.

To remember that "amar" means love, I place the famous magician Michael Ammar at the entrance to the mall. I imagine him large and colorful, and perhaps rather strangely (which is the point), he is pulling a beating heart from his magician's hat. The heart itself is large and colorful and pounding away. In fact, as it beats, I hear the sound "amar" over and over again.

Ayudar

Next, inside the mall, I want to place "ayudar," which means to help. Since Michael Ammar worked so well for "amar," I will recruit him for the rest of the words in this Memory Palace. **This is a very good trick.**

"Ayudar" has a strong "you/joo" sound in it, so I need to think about how to get an image from this. For whatever reason, YouTube comes instantly to mind, so I start to get an image of Ammar punching a laptop, one that is showing a video of Yoda helping Luke Skywalker cross a street that happens to be on the surface of the Death Star from Star Wars.

I want you to notice something here: I've been compressing a lot of images into a single space. They are vibrant and ridiculous to me, which means that they'll be memorable. However, reflecting upon them, I realize that I don't need

YouTube, because "Yoda" gives me the sound I need just as well as YouTube. Yoda can be further compressed with the Death Star, which helps me get the "dar" sound in "Ayudar."

My point here is, as you work on developing your associations do not hesitate to refine them. Adding on is just as important as taking away when it comes to the art of memory.

In my final image, I have Ammar punching Yoda as he is trying to help Ammar cross a street on the Death Star.

I'll have this image for as long as I want it and have "ayudar" as well.

Let's walk through one more example from the "A" Memory Palace.

Aprender

Let's learn the word for "to learn." It is "aprender." As it happens, the bookstore is the perfect place to put this word. This is one of those nice little "coincidences" you will find when you do memory work.

You will sometimes get words that are tricky like this. "Pren" brings nothing to mind other than a wren with a pen in its mouth. I don't like this, however, because the image meant to trigger the "P" sound comes after the image meant to give me "ren." (I automatically know that the word starts with "A" because it is stored in my "A" Memory Palace, further compounded by the fact that Michael Ammar is going to be in the picture just as soon as I can figure out how to fit him in). What I eventually decide to do with "aprender" is to have Michael Ammar "apprehended" by the police in front of the bookstore. Why? Because he is trying to steal of a copy of How to Learn & Memorize Spanish Vocabulary!

As always, I make everything huge and colorful and generally larger than life. The police are big and brutish in their blue uniforms and light sparkles from their badges, handcuffs and guns. Please note that "aprender" can also be used for "to memorize," but the normal word for that in Spanish would be "memorizar."

What About Memorizing Grammar?

This book does not purport to teach the memorization of grammar. However, I do have a few tips for the conjugation of verbs. This involves creating a special Memory Palace just for grammar rules.

So far, we have been dealing with Spanish verbs. This is where things can get tricky because you add a different ending to the verb depending on the gender and/or number of people speaking.

Verb Conjugation

Take, for instance, the Memory Palace that I use for conjugating verbs is the school where I teach. I use the kitchen, my office, the third classroom, the computer lab, the main hall, the second classroom, the reception desk, the first classroom, the front door, the outside hall, and the staircase (it's a small school). This school is particularly appropriate for me to use because my colleague who owns it is from Argentina and is a native Spanish-speaker.

Notice here that I have started in the kitchen because it is in the very back of the school. This way, I can move in a more-or-less straight line through the school without ever crossing my path or becoming trapped. Should I want to add more information to this particular Memory Palace, I have created it in such a way that I simply need to step out the door, walk past the veterinarians, the sun-tanning salon, the barbers, the dry cleaners, etc.

Before I describe how I use this particular Memory Palace to help remember grammar rules, let's take a brief look at verb conjugation in Spanish.

"Hablar," the word for "speak" usually appears first in most language trainings.

If you want to say, "I speak," you need to conjugate the word to "hablo."

If you want to say, "You speak," you need to conjugate the word to "hablas."

Likewise, "he speaks" and "she speaks" becomes "habla."

"We speak" needs "hablamos." "They speak" becomes "hablan." If you are referring to men or a group with men in it, you use "ellos hablan." If the group consists of women only, the term is "ellas hablan."

Let's apply this to "aprender."

I learn = aprendo (yo aprendo)

You learn = aprendes (tú aprendes)

He learns = aprende (el aprende)

She learns = aprende (elle aprende)

We learn = aprendemos (nosotros aprendemos)

They learn = aprendéis (vosotros aprendéis)

They learn = aprenden (ellos aprenden)

To remember that "I" usually ends with "o," I see myself in the kitchen jumping up and down on a box of cheerios.

To remember that "you" words usually end with either "as" or "es," I see myself pinning the tail on a donkey in my office.

To remember that "he" and "she" normally end with an "eh" sound, I see a Canadian saying, "What's up, eh!" in classroom number 3. He has a huge bottle of beer in his hand, and this itself says "eh" on it.

To remember that "we" usually ends with "os," I see myself with a group of students in the computer lab. "We" are marveling at the operating system on a new computer the school has purchased. It has a huge OS on the screen that is bursting with light to the point that it is burning our eyes.

To remember "they learn" is aprendéis/aprenden I have a dais in the hallway. This makes the hallway look a bit like a lecture hall, but it works. There is a lectern on the dais that says "the end" on it. This combined set of images worked marvelously when I was first trying to master this material.

Online Learning

 Empezemos! (Let's get started!) The quickest way to learn Spanish is by finding a teacher. If you can hire a one-on-one tutor, you should. Direct instruction, whether it be in a group class or with a private tutor, is one of the best ways to really pick up conversational Spanish. Also, having somebody that insists you to do homework and will hold you accountable can keep you on track. With an experienced tutor, you can receive guidance that's tailored to you providing a very structured approach to your personal goals. This is not the case with typical evening language classes where you will be expected to maintain the pace of the class; not very conducive to learning Spanish quickly.

This should be a fun endeavor for you, and the last thing you want is to end up in a stuffy class that takes away from the exciting discovery of new words and sentences. In most cases, these classes and tutors can be quite expensive, and since you're looking to learn quickly, you may not find many options available for the schedule you need. Take into consideration the commute as well. If you have Internet access, you can save yourself a lot of time and money.

If private tutoring and classes are out of the question, or if you want to continue learning outside of class, you can find everything you need on the internet, at the library, or at your local bookstore. Of course, if you have a smartphone, you have access to various instructional materials right at your fingertips.

There are plenty of both paid and free online websites and programs providing all varieties of instructional content for any level of Spanish student. You can find Podcasts, interactive websites, videos, and Apps. With so many options available, it can be challenging to decide which programs are right for you. Let's look at some of the most popular online resources available.

Podcasts

Podcasts are a great way to help build your skills as they allow you to hear native Spanish speakers. Listening to Podcasts can really maximize your learning since you're able to pick up on the pronunciation and phrases they commonly use. You can listen to a podcast while performing menial tasks and passively soak up the new knowledge.

When searching for the right Podcast for you, consider how long they've been on-air. Also, look for Podcasts that break down conversations slowly for beginners, so that you can understand them. While you can find Podcasts online for free, many require that you sign up or subscribe to a platform to access them.

Websites

If you prefer a more traditional approach to learning, some great websites have printable worksheets and interactive quizzes. While it is easy to find many websites that teach you the basics, it can be a challenge finding intermediate and expert Spanish level material. After you've committed some vocabulary to memory and can start stringing sentences together, check out websites that offer tests. Keep in mind most online testing will be focused on vocabulary and grammar; not necessarily speaking and listening. Practice typing in Spanish with websites that provide a Spanish keyboard that includes accents. That way, you can save time without having to figure out how to type those accents on your standard keyboard. Just perform a search for interactive websites for learning beginners Spanish and take your pick!

Videos

Diversify your Spanish instruction arsenal with videos. You shouldn't have a hard time locating hours of content online with sites such as YouTube. Be sure to bookmark your favorite videos so that you can find them easily when it's time to review. Videos work great because you can stop, pause, or rewind when needed. When watching videos, pay careful attention to pronunciation as well as study the mouth and lip movements of Spanish speakers. Closed-captioning can be a handy feature when listening to Spanish speakers — so that you can read along and start to develop an eye for the language as well. Try searching for a Spanish alphabet song, or even children's content showing numbers, colors, and nursery rhymes that you are already familiar with. Another fun way to get in practice time is to find Spanish games. There are a wide variety of games online, and you can search for games that will target your weakest areas. Reviewing your vocabulary and practicing your translation while under pressure or finding a fun game of simple matching can reinforce what you're learning offline.

Apps

There are many Apps available on your smartphone or tablet that are entirely free for use. Look for Apps that have a very straightforward interface and are easy to use. Using language Apps can help keep you motivated with goal-setting, visual cues to stay on track, and highlighting both strong and weak points. If you're interested in creating simple sentences right away, there are interactive Apps available to get you constructing phrases right away. Keep in mind that most Apps are not meant to be stand-alone courses, but they can make for a great addition to your learning toolbox. A simple internet search for top language apps will give you multiple lists with recommendations. Finding an app that supplies both visual and audio cues will be the most helpful, and you can even find Apps that have offline learning if you find yourself getting distracted online.

Focus on what you need

Because Spanish is considered one of the easiest languages for an English speaker to learn, you shouldn't have any trouble achieving success with a combination of online/offline materials. Even if you're not entirely convinced that you'll be able to pick up Spanish quickly these methods are available so that you can cut to the chase and focus on learning what you need. If you have any prior knowledge, you can build on what you already know and look forward to what you still need to learn.

While you don't want to overwhelm yourself with too much information, having a wide array available to stimulate new thoughts can really keep you on track. Keep away from materials loaded with grammar theory to start. Instead, try to find things that build your confidence; that could mean taking quizzes in workbooks or online. You need to see results fast so that you stay motivated and continue to be inspired. Develop a strategy so that you have access to the right tool when you need it. It can be easy to get discouraged and give up, just make sure that you always start again so that you do not forget everything that you've learned.

Surround Yourself

Immerse Yourself. At first, it can seem impossible to decipher the fast pace of native Spanish speakers. The series of staccato sounds makes it seem that they are speaking much faster than we do in English. How can we detect the patterns, rhythms, and nuances of the Spanish language? It is through immersing us in the language and paying attention to each sound that is made and how it relates to other sounds (and then practice making those sounds). Keep in mind that Spanish words run together, and when a word that begins with a vowel follows a word that ends with the same vowel, you only pronounce it once.

According to language theorist Stephen Krashen regarding acquiring a second language, you can gain language abilities through receiving messages that are only partially understood — which that are just above your current level of comprehension. That means that you can acquire the language subconsciously! This will also lead to gaining a greater understanding of Spanish speech rhythms.

Since language is a very regional thing, the goal here is to learn a standard variety that can be understood in all Spanish speaking areas. Learning grammar and phrasing will produce an unlimited number of meaningful sentences rather than only being able to pull from the phrases you have memorized. Keep in mind that memorizing function words and phrases will help you practice the framework of Spanish. So, how can you start immersing yourself in Spanish as a beginner? In addition to listening to Podcasts, you can watch movies, read books, listen to music, and literally surround yourself with the Spanish language. The goal here is to eat, speak, and dream in Spanish.

Spelling Rules in Spanish

Before beginning, it is important to clarify certain doubts about the pronunciation of some pairs of letters or phonemes in Spanish. In this language there are pairs of phonemes that are pronounced exactly the same but have different spelling, that is, the written letter is different. This case can be the phonemes /V/ and /B/ or also /LL/ and /Y/. In this lesson, dedicated to the basic rules of spelling, we will explain how each of these conflicting letters are used.

The use of 'P' and 'B'

When a P and B are in one word, and an N appears before them, this is replaced by M. This happens in all cases with no exception.

Covered

Amparado

The use of "V" and "B"

The letters B and V are not phonetically distinguished in Spanish. The two represent the bilabial sound / b /. On many occasions the reasons for using one or the other do not have a logical rationale that allows us to analyze the word and know which of them we are going to use, so there are times when you can only memorize the words that use them and those that do not use them. However, there are certain rules that will help:

Let's first talk about the letter B, this is used when a word

Beginning with: bibl- bio- sub

Library, biology, underwater.

Biblioteca, biología, submarino.

They begin with: ab- abs-ob, followed by a consonant;

Abdication, obsolete, obstetrics.

Abdicación, obsoleto, obstetricia.

They begin with the syllables: bu-bur-bus

Search, bular

Buscar, bular

When they have the prefixes: bien- bene

Welcome, benevolent

Bienvenido, benevolente

When they have the prefixes: bis- biz- bi

Great grandmother, bisexual, bicycle

Bisabuela, bisexual, bicicleta

When they end in: bundo- bunda- bilidad. With being
movilidad y civilidad the exception

Moribund, kindness

Moribundo, amabilidad

They end with: fobia- fobias -fobo - foba - fobos - fobas

Xenophobias, Claustrophobia.

Xenofobia, Claustrofobia.

When the words contain the sound / b / after an M

Ambulance

Ambulancia

When the words contain the sound / b / before the consonants L or R

Bracelet, bronchi, soft

Brazalete, bronquios, blando

The verbs beber, caber, deber, haber, saber and sorber. Also, its different conjugations and derivatives.

Verbs ending in -bir and -buir. Except for hervir, servir y vivir.

Write, attribute

Escribir, atribuir

Now we will talk about the use of the letter V:

When a word begins with -di. Dibujo and its derivatives being the exception

Divide, fun

Dividir, diversión

When a word begins with lla-lle-llo- llu.

Keychain, I will wear

Llavero, llevaré

When the word has the prefixes vice- viz-vi.

Viscount, viceroy

Vizconde, virrey

When the word contains the sound / b / after b, d, n;

Obvious, warning.

Obvio, advertencia.

When the word ends with the suffix -ívoro- ívora. Víbora being the exception

Carnivore, herbivore.

Carnívoro, herbívoro

When the word ends with -valencia -valente.

Prevalence, plurivalent.

Prevalencia, plurivalente.

The present indicative, the imperative and the subjunctive of the verb ir.

Go, go, go

Voy, ve, vaya

The past tense of the verbs whose infinitive does not contain B or V

Walk → I walked

Andar → anduve

The seasons of the year.

Spring Summer Winter.

Primavera, verano, invierno.

The use of "C", "S" and "Z"

First, we will begin with the use of C, its use varies according to each word. Normally its sound depends on the vowels A, O and U, for instance: casa, cosas, acuerdo.

Those words that end in z and are changed to the plural form are written with "C". Also, when the noun ends with TOR and in SOR, it changes to "CIÓN".

Pencil → pencils.

Lápiz → lápices.

Director → address.

Director → dirección.

We continue talking about the use of the S. All words ending in "SIVO" except for the words nocivo y lascivo. Also, the words that ends in: ES - ESA, ESCO, ESCA. Alteza being the exception to this rule. And finally, the adjectives that end in SIMO.

Intensive, depressive

Intensivo, depresivo

French

Francesa

Grotesque

Grotesca

Malísimo

Malísimo

The letter Z is used when words end in AZO: balazo. Also, with nouns ending in EZ - EZA. As you can see, it is difficult to determine in the latter when to place an S and when to place a Z. In this case there is no rule or analysis that you can follow, there are words that there is no choice but to learn them by heart.

Embrace

Abrazo

Nature

Naturaleza

Validity.

Validez.

The use of the "LL" and "Y"

The letter "LL" is used in words that begin with fa- fo- o fu. With the endings -alle -alle -ella -elle -ello -illa and -illo, except for: epopeya, plebeyo, zarigüeya, omeya. Finally, the words with verbal endings like -ellar, -illar, -ullar y -ullir and the verb hallar

Fail

Fallar

Beautiful

Bello

The letter "Y" is used to form the verbs ending in UIR.

Build

Construir

Verbal forms that do not use Y or LL in its infinitive form will be written using Y.

Go - go

Ir - vaya

Y will be written at the beginning of the yer sound.

Yerno, yerba.

Son-in-law, weed.

Y will be written after the ad, dis, sub sounds.

Adjacent, underlying.

Adyacente, subyacente.

The words that begin with yu are written with Y, except for the word lluvia and its derivatives.

Yucca, jugular.

Yuca, yugular.

The use of "G" and "J"

The letter G is used when:

The word has the prefix GEO- and is a compound word.

Geography, geometry.

Geografía, geometría.

The word has an ending in -GEN.

Origin, gene

Origen, gen

When the words have endings in -gélico, -genario, -géneo, -génico, -genio, -génito, -gesimal, -gésimo, -gético. Including their feminine and plural forms.

Homogeneous, ingenuity, quadragesimal.

Homogéneo, ingenio, cuadragesimal.

Words with endings in -gia, -gio, -gión, -gional, -gionario, -gioso and -gírico.

Magic, religion

Magia, religión.

When there is an ending -ger and -gir in the infinitive forms. Except for the verbs ejer, crujir and their derivatives.

Moo

Mugir

Speaking now about the letter J, when we progress more into Spanish you will have a couple of rules with which you can guide yourself, but it is good to remind you that many times there are no analysable reasons to understand a structure and you will have to use your memory to learn the correct writing of many words.

Words that end in -jería.

Counseling, locksmith.

Consejería, cerrajería.

In the tenses of the verbs whose infinitive bears that letter.

Crunch, work.

Crujir, trabajar.

The letter "Ñ"

The Ñ is a new letter for Spanish. To know its origin, we have to go back a few centuries ago, but not too many. We already know that Spanish is a romance language that comes from Latin, because this letter Ñ in Latin did not exist, it was a subsequent modification that was created in Spanish when it began to form and to evolve as a romance language along with Italian and French. In the ninth century the graphic representation of the Ñ was somewhat confusing, since it was a new letter that many began to improvise graphically. Instead of Ñ, it was more like: NN, GN.

But this letter was not born exclusively for Spanish, it turns out that in Galician and Asturian, it is also used, even some Aboriginal American languages also have this letter included in their alphabeticals. This of course, is an addition after the conquest of America.

The use of this letter has no rule subject to it, there are no regulations governing its appearance. Of course, this does not mean that it can be used randomly. The use of this letter, instead of its companions: The M and the N, totally changes the meaning of the words, for instance:

Bow - Monkey.

Moño - Mono.

Peña - Penalty.

Peña - Pena.

As with some other grammar rules, or simply, grammatical uses, the Ñ and its place within the words must be assigned to our memory. It is true that it can be very rough sometimes and it is difficult to sit down and think about all the lessons we have seen so far. However, remember that the practice makes perfect, that is why you will now have a great practices. Also remember to practice permanently since doing so once a week will not give the same results as you do it every day for at least 1 hour!

Bringing it All Together

Español	English
La navidad	Christmas
Vocabulario importante:	Important vocabulary:
activamente	actively
ancianos	elderly
cristiana	Christian
época	time
necesitadas	needy
pasar un buen tiempo	have a good time
paz	peace
pobres	poor
religioso	religious
voluntarios	volunteer

La navidad se celebra en muchos países del mundo. Esta celebración es principalmente de origen religioso. La navidad es la celebración del nacimiento de Jesucristo. Por lo tanto, existen muchas costumbres relacionadas con la religión cristiana.	Christmas is celebrated in many countries around the world. This celebration is mainly of religious origin. Christmas is the celebration of the birth of Jesus Christ. Therefore, there are many customs related to the Christian religion.
Pero la navidad también es una celebración familiar. La	But Christmas is also a family celebration. Christmas is an occasion where many

navidad es una ocasión en donde muchas familias se reúnen a pesar de vivir en diferentes países o incluso continentes. La navidad es una oportunidad para olvidarse de los problemas y pasar un buen tiempo juntos en familia y con amigos.

Otra de las características importantes de la navidad es la generosidad. En esta época, se practica la caridad. Muchas personas dan dinero a las obras de caridad como el Ejército de la Salvación. Estas organizaciones siempre están haciendo cosas positivas para personas pobres y necesitadas. Otras organizaciones están involucradas con niños y ancianos. Lo importante es ayudar a las personas que lo necesitan.

Quizá lo más conocido es el lado comercial de la navidad. Durante esta época, muchos negocios ponen ofertas especiales de ropa, electrónicos, juguetes y cualquier otro artículo. Si bien la navidad es una época para regalar cosas bonitas a la

families gather despite living in different countries or even continents. Christmas is an opportunity to forget about problems and have a good time together with family and friends.

Another important characteristic of Christmas is generosity. In this age, charity is practiced. Many people give money to charities like the Salvation Army. These organizations are always doing positive things for poor and needy people. Other organizations are involved with children and the elderly. The important thing is to help the people who need it.

Perhaps the best-known aspect is the commercial side of Christmas. During this time, many businesses have special offers on clothing, electronics, toys and many other items. While Christmas is a time to give beautiful things to family and friends, consumerism should not be familia y amigos queridos, el consumismo no debe ser la única razón para celebrarla.

Mi familia y yo celebramos la navidad en grande con todos nuestros amigos. Creemos que la navidad es una época para promover la paz y armonía entre todos. Hacemos nuestra contribución a las obras de caridad. No sólo damos dinero. También damos ropa, comida y ofrecemos nuestro tiempo como voluntarios. Es importante compartir con todos los que necesitan durante esta época tan maravillosa del año.

Si tú deseas apoyar obras de caridad, busca las que están trabajando activamente en tu comunidad. Seguramente hay organizaciones que están ayudando a muchas personas. Ellos te necesitan.

the only reason to celebrate it.

My family and I celebrate Christmas in grand fashion with all our friends. We believe that Christmas is a time to promote peace and harmony among all. We make our contribution to charities. We do not just give money. We also give clothes, food and volunteer our time. It is important to share with everyone who is needy during this wonderful time of the year.

If you want to support charitable organizations, look for those which are actively working in your community. Surely there are organizations that are helping many people. They need you.

Por favor responda las siguientes preguntas.	Please answer the following questions.
¿En dónde se celebra la navidad?	Where is Christmas celebrated?
_____ _____ _____ _____ _____ _____	_____ _____ _____ _____ _____ _____
¿Qué es la navidad?	What is Christmas?
_____ _____ _____ _____ _____ _____	_____ _____ _____ _____ _____ _____

¿Para qué es una oportunidad la navidad? _____ _____ _____ _____ _____ _____ _____ _____	What is Christmas an opportunity for? _____ _____ _____ _____ _____ _____ _____
¿Cuál es otra de las características importantes de la navidad? _____ _____ _____ _____ _____ _____ _____ _____	What is another important characteristic of Christmas? _____ _____ _____ _____ _____ _____ _____

¿Para quién hacen cosas positivas las organizaciones?	For whom do organizations do positive things?
_____ _____ _____ _____ _____ _____ _____	_____ _____ _____ _____ _____ _____
¿Cómo celebramos la navidad en mi familia?	How do my family and I celebrate Christmas?
_____ _____ _____ _____ _____ _____ _____ _____	_____ _____ _____ _____ _____ _____

Respuestas sugeridas	Suggested answers

¿En dónde se celebra la navidad?	Where is Christmas celebrated?
La navidad se celebra en muchos países del mundo.	Christmas is celebrated in many countries around the world.
¿Qué es la navidad?	What is Christmas?
La navidad también es una celebración familiar.	Christmas is also a family celebration.
¿Para qué es una oportunidad la navidad?	What is Christmas an opportunity for?
La navidad es una oportunidad para olvidarse de los problemas y pasar un buen tiempo juntos en familia y con amigos.	Christmas is an opportunity to forget about problems and have a good time with family and friends.
¿Cuál es otra de las características importantes de la navidad?	What is another important characteristic of Christmas?
Otra de las características importantes de la navidad es la generosidad.	Another important characteristic of Christmas is generosity.
¿Para quién hacen cosas positivas las organizaciones?	For whom do organizations do positive things?
Para las personas pobres y necesitadas.	For poor and needy people.

¿Cómo celebramos la navidad en mi familia?	How do my family and I celebrate Christmas?
Celebramos la navidad en grande con todos nuestros amigos.	We celebrate Christmas in grand fashion with all of our friends.

CONCLUSION

We've finally reached the end of this book and I sincerely would like to congratulate you on making it this far. I hope you found the learning experience enjoyable and rewarding. And I hope that you continue using Spanish movies, TV shows, and music to reach your ultimate Spanish speaking goals. As you continue using this method and immersing yourself in the Spanish culture, I'm confident you'll be speaking fluently in no time! I wish you the very best of luck! Thank you for picking up our book to learn and study with. Until next time! ¡Buena suerte!

We communicate every day through conversations, phone calls, social media, text, and emails. Interaction is how we communicate and exchange ideas. So, you might say that language is inherently interactive. We may define interaction as two people or things that have an influence or affect each other. In this context, it is two or more people exchanging ideas and information and influencing each other positively.

When interacting with a proficient speaker, you get a chance to ask questions in areas that you haven't understood. It helps you in the comprehension of the language. Interactions of this kind help in language facilitation, and evidence will be seen in the long run as your grammar accuracy and Spanish fluency improve.

Thank you for taking the time to study and read through this book. I hope the conversations and vocabulary included have been as useful to you as they have been for me. They certainly have helped me in my travels throughout Latin America. In fact, these kinds of dialogues, phrases, and expressions have helped me make new friends, move around, ask for help, and socialize in various contexts. For instance, I've made plenty of new friends in local shops, markets, and restaurants by simply being able to greet people, ask for their name and give them my basic information. From there, I was able to take the conversations even further by asking what their hobbies were, what kind of music they liked, what they did for fun, etc.

Now that you have finished the book, we hope that you really liked it, and you have enjoyed and learned a lot with the words written here, we carefully chose and used each word so you could maximize your learning.

Felicitaciones, ya debes ser capaz de entender esta frase.

The next step to reach a more advanced level of the Spanish language would be to write about your daily activities using the sentences written here as a basis. To have an advanced level of the Spanish language is extremely important to study the verb tenses of the Spanish language because there are many more than those existing in English.

Once again, we want to remind you that this is not a book that you should read only once because it has a lot of content, and it is difficult to learn the first time you read it.

Hasta luego, sigue practicando tu español y muy pronto verás lo fácil que es.

Lightning Source UK Ltd.
Milton Keynes UK
UKHW020655210521
384116UK00005B/137